# LIVE IN IT

"Ignited in Your Purpose"

BY SHALANNA S. BLADES

# CONTENTS

Day 1: Get Out the Boat — 12

Day 2: He Loves Me, He Loves Me Not — 18

Day 3: What is in Your House — 24

Day 4: No Checked Baggage: Liabilities Get Left Behind — 29

Day 5: I Said Amen...Now What? — 35

Day 6: God Secured the Bag—YOU! — 42

Day 7: Peace in the Midst of Chaos — 46

Day 8: Take Your Hands Out of the Cookie Jar — 51

Day 9: The Weight of Waiting — 56

Day 10: Fill Your Tank — 61

Day 11: When Delay Looks Like No—Endure Patiently — 65

**Day 12:** Unauthorized Gap Fillers     70

**Day 13:** Be. Humble.     74

**Day 14:** Resurrected Vision:     80
Dream Again

**Day 15:** Power of Now     84

**Day 16:** From This to That     89

**Day 17:** The Benediction: Keys to     94
Evolving in Your Purpose

# THANKS

I dedicate this book to my paternal grandparents, Sylvia Jones, and Victor Joseph Blades; my cousin, Jevorn Herbert; and my inherited father, Alfonsa "Samp" Meredith; all of whom have transitioned into glory. Their love for life and adventure are constant reminders to continue to breathe in gratitude and breathe out purpose!

But a special dedication for this labor of love goes out to my deceased maternal grandma, Veronica Thomas. She taught me the greatest gift we could ever give is a generous heart filled with love. I am who I am because of her. With her abundant pearl of wisdom, she always said, "Your hands must always be free." I love you, Grandma; you will forever be my queen. My hands will always be free to give and to love.

Special thanks to my family for their continued love and support - even when the leading of God in my life looked like I was all over the place. Great thanks to my prayer and accountability partners (you all know who you are) who pushed me to live in my purpose when all I wanted to do was settle for what seemed less painful. A heartfelt gratitude goes out to my parents, Christine "Jenny" Blades and Francis "Junior" Blades for anchoring me when I felt broken and lost as I pilgrimaged through life. And last, but not least, thanks to our Heavenly Father for staying true to His word; for opening and closing doors to propel me into my calling, and for the countless times of correction in love. My gratitude is an outpour of my love for all of you! THANK YOU!

# The Prelude: Ready, Set, Start

Welcome to the journey of fulfilling your God-given purpose. My mission is to be a purpose partner to aide all who read this devotional and desire to be ignited in his/her purpose through the spiritual journey of trusting God. The foundation of living a purpose-filled life is having faith in God wholeheartedly. In order to "live in it", you must give yourself permission to fail (first attempt in learning), remember God qualifies the unqualified, relinquish control over to Him, and envision your purpose. Allowing yourself to fail does not mean you live your life recklessly. Instead, it is you creating space for experiential learning from within and influential leading from our Heavenly Father to unveil you as His masterpiece. You ask, "What does it mean to give myself over to God?" It literally means taking your hands (human intellect) off the situation. It means being flexible to God's leading as you release yourself from thoughts of doubt and fear; generally birthed out of unfavorable past life circumstances. When you have a clear vision of your purpose you gain focus which breathes life into your goals. You already heard God's word for your life. Now it is time to *live in it*!

    Why am I here? Why do you I feel stuck in this cycle in life? Have you ever asked yourself these questions throughout your adult life? Trust me, I have asked myself this question so many times. I started to believe I was created to have a mediocre life of "adulting". At one point in my life, I felt like a slave to a computer wasting eight plus hours a day keying in data and spewing out reports. "God is this all to life – to be stuck in a confined space with low ceilings and no windows; crunching numbers with little to no human interaction?" It was a cry for relief. Inquiring of God about my purpose was far from my mind during this 'pit' season of my life. I just wanted out! Honestly, I failed to realize that my current position was not my purpose; it was my preparation. I believe sometimes we feel stagnant in a cycle of mere existence because we have allowed a job, a circumstance, or an unmet desire for significance to define us. Your purpose is not always your position, but God uses your position to promote you into your purpose. Your purpose will go through seasons along with position changes. Your purpose will never change because it is the reason why God created you, but it will evolve. Many will think their purpose changed or they heard incorrectly from God overtime because of the pressure from outside factors. That sensing is a symptom of a season. That feeling of plateau or staleness with little direction or outlook to what is next are a clear indication that God is calling you to the threshing floor (your prayer closet if you will). Remember, your purpose is a living constant, such as our Heavenly Father, it does not change. It grows. If you feel a shifting in your life, seek God for direction for the next elevation steps to operate in your calling.

As a result of my own plateau, this collection of faith experiences involving family, friends—and more importantly, me; came this seventeen-day trust walk journey with God. Many of us know our respective purposes, but we wrestle with the process. As you commit to these seventeen days, my desire is that you trust in the finished work on the cross. Your faith will be the transfer of trust. In the Hebraic language the number seventeen represents "overcoming the enemy" and "complete victory". I declare that each of you will overcome the enemy and have complete victory in living in your purpose. The foundational scripture for the Live in It challenge is **Psalm 143:8 New Living Translation** version:

*"Let me hear of Your unfailing love each morning, for I am trusting You. Show me where to walk, for I give myself to You."*

This verse will be your declaration each day over the next seventeen days. You will not only read it but will say it out loud with **authority to command your day under God's guidance.** When you speak mountains move! God *spoke* the Earth into existence. Through salvation He has given us the same power to speak our desires into existence. In addition to audibly stating your daily declaration, **aligning your state of being - mental and body - for this journey will be vital.** Detox yourself of things you may watch on television and social media, listen to on the radio or on other virtual mediums. Also, plan to eat healthily during this time. Getting a full night's rest is critical for this journey because it positions your mind and body to fully receive what God is going to be downloading in your spirit. Positively change how you see and feel about yourself, and actively reshape your perspective. Incorporate a set time for meditation to be at rest in your mind; to be still in the presence of God. Meditate by having scriptures read out loud from a recording, light gospel music playing in the background, and or nature sounds that will bring you to a posture of tranquility. Each day you will need your

Bible to find relevant scriptures and a journal to write down your responses for the following reflection questions listed below:

1. What am I grateful to God for today?
2. How did I "Live in It" for my purpose today?
3. What did today's chapter reveal to me?
4. Did I allow God to be in control or did I allow myself to be my own God today? How did I or how did I not surrender control?

Finally, pray that God shows you who will be your prayer and/or accountability partner for your "Live in It" experience. Discovering and walking in your purpose is not a solo journey. There will be times of deep reflection that will require you to be transparent with someone who is called to run this race with you, who loves not only you, but the God in you. After each day's reading, there is a suggested song strategically chosen to set the atmosphere for your intimate time of devotion with the Lord. You can select any music listening platform to play it.

You, the one reading this book right now, need to know that my prayer partners and I have covered you in prayer countlessly. I will continue to lift your purpose before the King of kings and Lord of lords. My prayer is that your spiritual eyes be open to God's vision for your life and that you be an active participant in His will for you. You will not give up; you will cast all your cares upon God and speak life daily as a beacon of light for God's Kingdom. Understand that God has sent His Son to free all mankind from the bondage of a life of emptiness purposelessness. When you walk in your purpose you walk in the power God has given you to live an abundant life. Always remember *you are anointed for your purpose!*

# PREFACE

*"You may not be able to walk on water, but even man has survived the fire. The process, your journey, is necessary so that you can fully be grateful of the success"*
LaTonya Roberts, Founder of LTR LLC, La MSM, LSSBB, ITIL, MBTI

My aha...

What does a seventeen-year-old know about heartbreak? You would be surprised. At the tender age of seventeen I experienced my first relationship heartache. Yes, I said first, but I did not say only. That moment in my life was a defining moment. Matter of fact, it was the best thing that could have ever happened to me because it was the catalyst that led me to move thousands of miles from home to Greensboro, North Carolina. It was there I would proudly attend the illustrious North Carolina Agricultural and Technical State University. It was there I discovered Shalanna and was introduced to my purpose. It was not until several years later I would begin to live in it.

God reveals "aha" moments that are aligned to your purpose throughout your life. The reason you had to be on that job with a bitter manager, be rejected by the one you gave your heart to, or be stuck in a perceived wilderness in life were all divinely orchestrated to present you with your God-given purpose. Your purpose makes you come to life. Your purpose gives meaning to life. When you consider your voyage of existence, you will begin to connect the dots with a newfound appreciation for your process.

Be reflective. Become more. Protect your peace. Get in God's word daily.

### Prayer for the reader

*Gracious and merciful Father let the words of my mouth and the meditation of my heart be acceptable in Your sight, O Lord, my strength, and my Redeemer. Abba Father, I praise and worship Your awesome name. Holy Spirit I pray Your presence to be ushered into the occupied space in which the one currently reading this book is located. I pray the reader has a desire to have an open heart and mind to receive every specific thing You would have for them to embrace in this season. Pour out a fresh anointing. I declare a special blessing of unprecedented favor to surround the reader as a mighty shield. Remind the reader of your everlasting and unconditional love that never falters. May Your goodness be made known. I declare great success as You deem it God in every area of the reader's life. In Jesus' name; amen.*

DAY 1

# Get Out the Boat

*"Trust in the LORD with all your heart; and lean not to your own understanding."*
– Proverbs 3:5 NLT

Here you are. Your heart is racing. Your palms are sweating. You faintly hear the word, "come." "Come my child," He whispers. Come? God, seriously? How will this work? How is this possibly going to happen? How will I explain this to people? "Do You not see the chaos in my situation? Each one of these questions may arise when God calls you to level up and activate your faith in Him. We sail along life in this 'boat' of false protection in efforts to shield ourselves from disappointment. It feels safe to not rock the boat by stepping out on faith and trusting God in what you know in your heart you are supposed to do. Nonetheless, getting out of the boat moves you from independence to dependence on Him. It requires trusting God as He launches you out into the deep. Our precious minds have become housing for negative thoughts of doubt and fear; so much so, it leaves little to no room for positive thoughts to dwell. This very same fear robs us of joy and turns our purposes into seemingly unattainable fairytales. In the Bible, God tells us in the book of Philippians chapter four verse eight to fix our thoughts on what is true, and honorable, and right, and pure, and lovely, and admirable. All these things are excellent and worthy to give God praise. Operating in faith creates the opportunity to do something that you have never done or seen before in your lifetime. I know for me I have dipped my foot over the side of the boat testing the water so to speak - halfway in halfway out. This was disobeying God's command to "come" just as He instructed Peter in the storm (*read Matthew 14:22-33*). God did not ask me to analyze His command for it to make sense in my carnal mind; nor is He asking you to do the same today. Walking in your purpose is a true faith walk because naturally we want to make logical sense of everything that is presented to us in efforts to eliminate any potential hardship. Placing our trust into what we cannot physically see or touch (such as God) can create this element of fear of failure, pain, and/or loss. Many of you live a life so entangled with risk-avoidance. I like to call it living an anxious-driven life dominated by taking calculated risks. It is in the risk aversion you get consumed with fear in which you begin to live a life of avoidance instead of advancement. You then become so crippled by fear you do not pursue what you are called to do in your purpose. The vision is given, but all the steps are generally not nicely laid out like a 10-step success plan as we would expect. Steps make sense, but it does not make faith. It is fair to say that this notion can be an unsettling feeling to entrust your heart to an unseen God you know who is there, but question whether will really be there for you. Getting out of the boat is trusting God fully with our respective purposes to get us to our divine destinies. Getting out of the boat represents a high-risk investment with the highest dividend return. It is relinquishing control to a Heavenly Being you cannot physically see or touch. It is setting your heart before His presence to find strength in His rest. It is hearing God say, "Trust me in this; I will order your steps."

What is causing you to stay in the boat instead of launching out into the deep? Is it fear? Is it laziness? Is it lack of vision? Ask yourself, "Is the fear of the unknown worth living a mediocre and disobedient life deprived of the overflow that comes from anchoring my faith in what God has called me to do? Is wallowing in procrastination creating a false sense of security in the borrowed time I have on this Earth?" Are your eyes so fixated on everything you see physically that you are blinded spiritually? Or, are you stuck in a characteristic pattern that is rooted in something deeper than what meets the eye? The reason why you can trust God when you cannot trace Him is because of His proven track record. His heart towards you is incomprehensible. We may not see nor understand God's hand, but we know His heart. Either you are going to be a victim of the enemy or victor of the Lord. Ask God to forgive you now for restructuring His instructions to you with your reasoning because it has caused you to operate outside of His perfect will for your life. We cannot use our finite minds to understand God's infinite ways. Yes, the process may look grim and crazy; but on the other side of it is your destiny. The first step to walking in your purpose starts with one word—come.

Why live a watered-down version of yourself? Familiarity creates an entrapment of being less than what God has called you to be. At the end of your comfort zone you will find the blessings of faith. As we commune with God, He will help us to refocus our thoughts. The demands of life have moved our hearts away from His personal invitation to come join Him out of the boat. Personally speaking, I could feel the weight of the obstacles in my life, but I got so comfortable with carrying them to the point they became my identity. I became, Shalanna "I am stuck" Blades. I found myself rationalizing next steps I needed to take as it related to my purpose. The thing that God told me, and I am telling you now is, "You have to stop denying what I have for you with your delay." Choose purpose over procrastination. Launch out into the deep! Jump!

**Daily Declaration**
"Let me hear of Your unfailing love each morning, for I am trusting You. Show me where to walk, for I give myself to You."

**Prayer**
Heavenly Father, I cast out fear and doubt for they are not of You. I give You my hand and my heart to lead me into the deep for You are my Protector and Provider. For You are Elohenu Olam, Everlasting God, that existed before time and will experience no end. I confess my finite mind cannot grasp the totality of your power and

greatness, but I submit my yes unto you. Your promises are "yes and amen". Renew my mind oh God so that it is fixed on whatever is true, noble, right, pure, lovely, and admirable. I will be obedient and not sit in the shallow end of what you have called me to do. Change my perspective to relish in the journey of completely trusting You. Share Your secrets with me, oh God. As I hear You calling me to come away with You, give me peace to follow You wholeheartedly. I know in Your presence there is great peace. In Your loving arms I find rest. Strengthen me Lord until I know You; until I know Your love for me. I will soar with You above the dark clouds. Forgive me for worrying and not trusting in Your wisdom and power that only You, the everlasting God, have in all of creation. I love You Elohenu Olam. In Jesus' name, amen.

**Today's Song Selection**
"Oceans" - Hillsong UNITED


**Moment of Reflection**
1. What am I grateful to God for today?
2. How did I "Live in It" for my purpose today?
3. What did today's chapter reveal to me?
4. Did I allow God to be in control or did I allow myself to be my own God today? How did I or how did I not surrender control?

blessings of faith
Either you are going to be a Victim of the enemy or a Victor of the Lord.
COMFORT ZONE
DAY 1: get out of the boat
JOY
FEAR
NEGATIVE THOUGHTS
DOUBT
divine destinies
trusting God
dependance on Him
INDEPENDENCE
FALSE PROTECTION

DAY 2

# He Loves Me, He Loves Me Not

*"Let me hear of your unfailing love each morning, for I am trusting you. Show me where to walk, for I give myself to you."*
*Psalm 143:8 NLT*

God uniquely created each of us in His image; not to compare ourselves to others, but to delight in His masterpiece. He loves you just as He created you.

Have you ever questioned God's love for you? Wondered if He even cared that you were struggling while everybody around you appeared to be prospering and living the life? You, my friend, have stumbled upon one of the oldest tricks of the enemy: magnifying a current circumstance and/or comparing another person's "perfect life" status to create doubt about God's love for us. Sometimes we may question God's love for us in His silence. Typically, we equate silence with being dismissed and/or ignored. It is in God's precious silence where He checks our hearts toward Him and brings about the greatest manifestation of His promised word. God is vested in giving us the very desires of our hearts through our diligence in seeking Him. Do not be dismayed or apathetic in the silence. He uses this time to strengthen our understanding of why we were created and who our Creator is to us. His silence connects us with God in a deeper manner through the Holy Spirit. Living in your purpose requires a high-level of understanding of not only knowing who you are, but Whose you are.

    I used to refer to myself as the "red-headed stepchild" of the Kingdom because I felt that I would have to fight insurmountable battles only to get a trickling of blessings while others experienced a cake-walk process and received a *downpour* of the floodgates of blessings. It is crazy how the devil loves to play with our minds and disrupts our faith in God. Know that the devil is after your faith; your faith in God is the lifeline to pleasing Him and moving forward in your purpose. Our faith is the activation of our hope. You frustrate the devil when you fight with faith in God's word instead of with fear from internal words which try to immobilize you. Of course, my perception of God's love for me (or lack thereof) was inaccurate and created a wall of distrust towards God and His word. As you embrace your purpose, you must know that God loves you! You have the exact measure of faith that is needed to believe you are chosen by God's love to bulldoze through the wall of distrust. This truth of being chosen cannot be a passive acceptance. Wholeheartedly *receive* God's love by being in His presence through prayer, meditation, and study of His word fervently. Make it your lifestyle. This develops a close relationship with God to know His heart towards you, which will be an ongoing lesson. Like any loving relationship, transparency and vulnerability are key components needed to fully open your heart to embrace God's love. To go through life without intimacy with the Father is to miss the very essence of your existence. God's love is everlasting and steadfast; it is how we discover our identity. As you walk in your purpose, it is critical that you know the character of God. To know God's character is to know God's heart. To know God's heart is to know God's love. Study Isaiah 41:10 and let it resonate with you.

Knowing God's character deepens your understanding of God's love for His children and how He works in accordance with His written word. Romans 5:8 says, *"But God demonstrates His own love for us in this while we were still sinners Christ died for us."* You no longer need to play the "He loves me; He loves me not" pull-the-petals-off-of-the-flower game to determine whether or not God loves you because He loves you—*period.* There are going to be times in your life you may question God's love because of the intense external factors surrounding you; leaving you feeling hopeless. When we doubt God, we must be honest about our feelings and our questions. Tell Him. Be so transparent with God about your reservations about having faith in Him and His word. It is in that level of transparency God can restore your hope, clear your vision, and unclog your heart so you can fully receive His love. Begin saying (even right now as you read this), "God loves me". Repeat it over and over to establish it in the atmosphere and engrave it on your heart. This is not hype, this is hope! The depth of our faith in God depends on our depth of our knowledge of God's love for us. Some of us struggle in our faith in God's love when it appears He is muted to our situation. Know that God's silence is His way of allowing His perfect work to take its rightful place in your life; allowing you to develop in your trust-walk with Him. Although you may go through a season of feeling forsaken by our Heavenly Father, you will grow to understand that He is better to you than anyone has ever been. Your faith is being strengthened in the silence in order stay the course of your purpose. Commit to stay in His presence regardless of the trials. You refuel by reconnecting to the Father. Remember a teacher never speaks to his/her students during the test!

God's love is not like mankind's love. Often, we mistake the nature of God's love by our experience with people who profess their love for us but mistreat us. We cannot hold God to other's actions. The kind of love our Heavenly Father has for us is protective, corrective, and redemptive. His love protects us from weapons of this world *(read Isaiah 54:17)*. His love corrects us when we have strayed away from the obedient path *(read Hebrews 12:6)*. His love redeems us by the power of Jesus's blood; making us victorious over the schemes of the enemy *(read Ephesians 1:7-10)*. I have wrestled with this "God loves me" notion for years because of the insecurity of not being enough, disappointment and abandonment. I viewed God through fragmented lenses that reflected my brokenness, and not my blessings. In His Fatherly way, He continuously shows me His love to tear down my protective self-made wall I built around my heart. Some of you may resonate with this feeling. Do you know that God knew you before He formed you in your mother's womb *(Jeremiah 1:5)*? Every hurt, shame, success, misstep was the fuel to our purposes. Our whole existence matters because our lives got purpose. Purpose is the answer to a problem. Your purpose is the solution to a problem only your existence can solve. I know you may be reading this and thinking to yourself, "Okay; yeah right. I am no one special. I did not solve world hunger or something major on that level!" Sure, you may not be the 21st Century Gandhi, but you may be a parent who is raising future leaders who will positively impact the world because of the wisdom you constantly sow into them. Maybe you are the kind-hearted person who decided to spark up a conversation with a stranger on the way to work; not knowing that stranger's yearning for acceptance led to suicidal thoughts. But because of your kindness this stranger decided to give life a try again and becomes a renowned doctor advocating for mental health. A distinguish platform, accolades, or a string of letters after your name do not dictate whether you got purpose. God's love gave you purpose. You were created to be an answer to a problem. Accepting the true love of God is the doorway to abundantly loving God's creation called *you*!

**Daily Declaration**
"Let me hear of Your unfailing love each morning, for I am trusting You. Show me where to walk, for I give myself to You."

**Prayer**
Dear Abba Father, I come before You asking to be restored in my faith. El Hayyay, God of my life, pour into me where I have been depleted by the antics of this world and people. I have allowed

fear and doubt to taint my perspective of Your love for me. I know You love and adore me Father because You show it time and time again. Today, I decide to walk in that faith—to put it to work in the situations around me that I cannot control. I commit myself to operate in mountain-moving faith, for I know that it is impossible to please You without it according to Hebrews 11:6. No longer will I question Your love for me. I cast out down arguments and every high thing that exalts itself against the knowledge of God, bringing every thought into captivity to the obedience of Christ. I am the apple of Your eye because You first chose me. This I pray in Jesus' name. Amen.

**Today's Song Selection**
"You are Loved" - Stars Go Dim

**Moment of Reflection**
1. What am I grateful to God for today?
2. How did I "Live in It" for my purpose today?
3. What did today's chapter reveal to me?
4. Did I allow God to be in control or did I allow myself to be my own God today? How did I or how did I not surrender control?

DAY 3

# What is in Your House

*"By his divine power, God has given us everything we need for living a godly life. We have received all of this by coming to know him, the one who called us to himself by means of his marvelous glory and excellence."*
*2 Peter 1:3 NLT*

Did you know that everything you need is right inside of you? When you accepted Jesus Christ as your Lord and Savior, He took residence inside of you. He sent the Holy Spirit to be your comforter and guide to have a mind governed by the Spirit which is life and peace *(read Romans 8:2-6)*. Many of us think we must hold a certain amount of prestigious degrees and honors or be connected to specific professional or social networks to make life advancements. Those things are great resources and important at some level professionally, but it does not supersede what is already in your "house". God masters in using people, things, and situations that the world would consider to be unqualified. Due to this, many of

God's people feel inadequate and search for personal enhancements to fulfill an innate God-given desire. God is saying, "My precious child, I never do an incomplete job. When I created you, I made you complete before I placed you in your mother's womb. Accepting My Son, Jesus Christ, was the internal awakening to every good and perfect gift necessary for you to fulfill your purpose. Do not shortchange yourself by seeking anything but Me, Your Father. Stay at My feet; I will show you great and mighty things with the move of My hands and the leading of the Holy Spirit. I have spoken. Just say yes!"

I think of the widower in *2 Kings 4* who was left in debt upon the death of her husband. Notice that two things were deceased at the same time: her finances and her love life—two things we know that can terribly disrupt anyone's world. The prophet Elisha asked her what she had in her possession to be used to create wealth for her household. She stated that all she had was one jar of oil. Elisha stirred up a great expectation within this woman's heart and mind when he told her to gather many empty vessels from all her neighbors. This expectation exceeded what she physically had, but her obedience with the little she had created her overflow of blessing. She was instructed to shut the door behind her after gathering those plentiful vessels. The significance of mentioning this command to close the door in the verse is to demonstrate how to protect what God has spoken directly to us. Everybody outside of our respective houses does not need access to what God is doing inside our houses (inside of us). Outside chatter from others can breed doubt and fear which can taint what we have inside of us to be successful in what

God has purposed for us to do. It can even delay our progression. This widower thought her world was over when her husband – the sole provider of the home—was dead and what was needed to live seemed to be dead, too. God sent Elisha, His servant, to remind this woman that though her earthly resources were gone the great Source, God, would not only meet her need, but He would teach her how to maintain the overflow of abundance. I believe this is what God is reminding all of us now; although a familiar means to meet a need may change, God's unchanging fatherly love moves Him to partner with us to uncover a sustainable solution for that need.

God created each one of us on purpose with purpose for a purpose. Your unique DNA tells you who you are, a - Divine Noble Achiever. This means your life is intentionally equipped to bring forth something of superior quality in this world that no one else can do except for you. Take care of your "house" for in it holds precious treasures that only you possess. God has made you a finished work. Your seasons of preparation have made you well-equipped to excel in your purpose. It is already in you!

**Daily Declaration**
"Let me hear of Your unfailing love each morning, for I am trusting You. Show me where to walk, for I give myself to You."

**Prayer**
Gracious and merciful God. Thank You for gifting me with everything I need to walk in the fullness of my purpose. Jehovah Jireh, my Provider, I want for nothing. Help me not to look to my left

nor my right as if I am lacking the essentials to complete everything You have called me to do. I declare that everything that I shall touch prospers and benefits not only myself, but those connected to me. Just as the widow in debt obeyed your servant by sending out her sons to collect empty vessels amongst their neighbors in order to pour out the little oil she had left in her house; so will I pour out all that is within me until the flow ceases at the appointed time. I am well able and equipped to endure the process of my purpose with excellence because I have power! I am a great steward over my purpose. It is in the mighty name of Jesus' name I pray boldly unto You mighty God. Amen.

Today's song selection
"Good Good Father" - Chris Tomlin ft. Pat Barrett

**Moment of Reflection**
1. What am I grateful to God for today?
2. How did I "Live in It" for my purpose today?
3. What did today's chapter reveal to me?
4. Did I allow God to be in control or did I allow myself to be my own God today? How did I or how did I not surrender control?

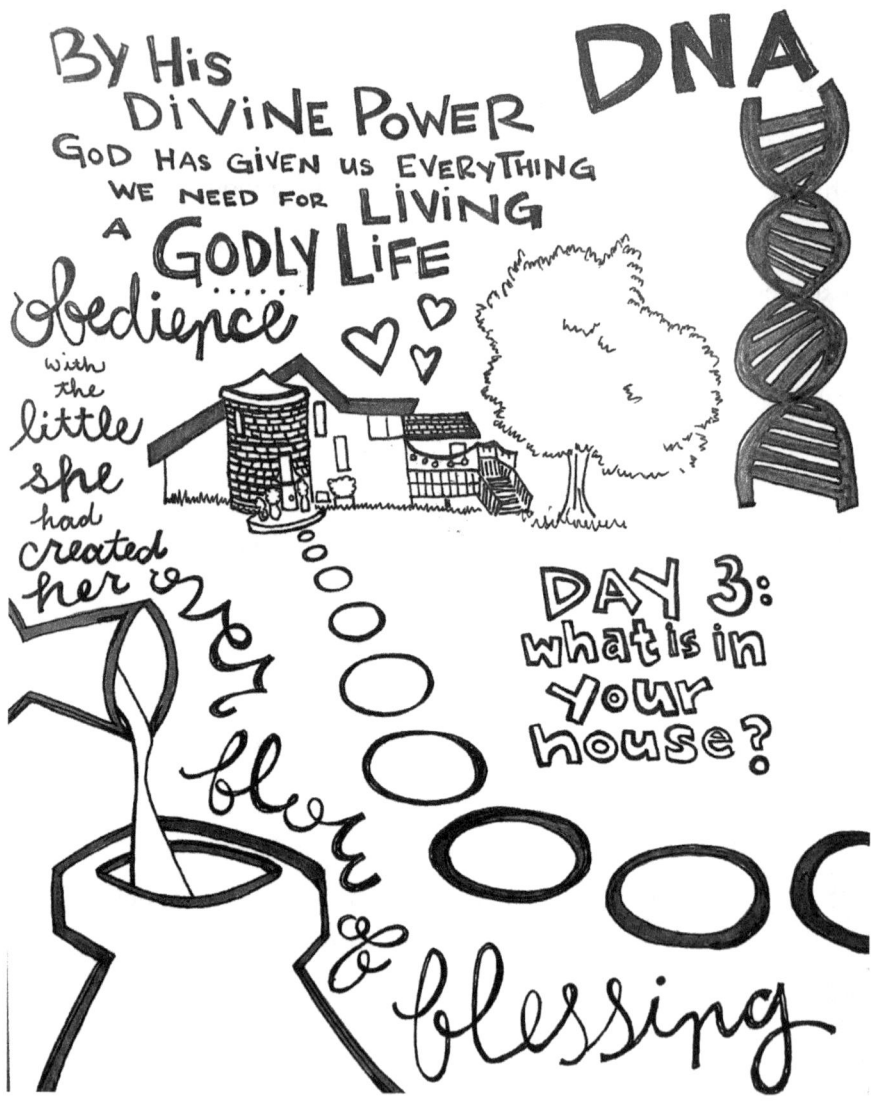

DAY 4

# No Checked Baggage: Liabilities Get Left Behind

*"Those who trust their own insight are foolish, but anyone who walks in wisdom is safe."*
Proverbs 28:26 NLT

Liabilities can be weapons of mass distraction. Nothing delays or kills your vision faster than the unnecessary baggage that can come from the people who are in your inner circle and/or the lifestyle you choose to live based on the decisions you make. Often time people will think just because he/she is not living a reckless lifestyle then accountability (in other words, submission) unto God is not a factor. Not only is this notion ignorant, it is a dangerous path of foolishness.

Safeguarding yourself from excessive setbacks is wisdom exemplified. You do this when being selective with whom you give VIP backstage access to your heart which is a direct entry into your mind and soul). Stop and think. Who are you giving your ear to? What seeds are you allowing to be sown in your soil (spirit) by maintaining unfruitful relationships? Is having this person around beneficial for your vision or detrimental to it? Are you living a life holy and acceptable before the Father? More than ever, we are living in a self-serving society in which people value what they can get from you. For instance, people will witness your relationship with God and observe how your unique connection to the Vine results in visible blessings. As they observe your relationship with the Lord, some may be compelled to leech onto you and suck away your anointing because it is easier to take instead of develop what is necessary to activate their own God-given anointing. This can create a dependency that will leave you feeling depleted. That feeling of exhaustion can become a setback in your progression. Sadly, there are some people who surround you who are not for you, but for your stuff. They know the advantage is in you. They want to steal what you have and act as if it is their own. You are a carrier of God's light which projects a peaceful attraction. This attraction may bring people into your life who may not know how to handle your illumination. People mistreat what they do not value.

Some of our connections with other people can be a liability to our purpose. Take inventory of who are significant influencers in your life. Now ask yourself, how do these individuals support me? Do they celebrate my steps toward fulfilling my purpose, do they correct me in my mishaps, and/or do they encourage me when negative thoughts try to overshadow my destiny? Please note, everyone will not understand your purpose because the vision was not given to them. In their failure to comprehend the direction of your life, they may "throw shade" which may be perceived as a form of rejection. But I say to you, no longer take ownership of others' impaired vision causing you to be entangled by the snares of their rejection. We are first and foremost chosen by God. Even Jesus was rejected by His own people. Despite His experience, He died for them and the rest of mankind because of His ultimate purpose to reunite us back to our Creator. To be fit for your purpose journey, you cannot have unnecessary amounts of time managing other people's feelings and/or opinions. This becomes a mental liability draining you physically; cutting off your motivation to keep pressing forward. Sometimes you must disconnect to connect. Disconnect from the things that are preventing you from connecting to God through praying and fasting. Always remember God specifically gave you the vision of your purpose. Therefore, people cannot be surrogates to *your* vision-baby. It is for *you* to carry and for *you* to deliver at God's appointed time!

We are created to be interdependent with each other in a healthy manner that does not take advantage of one another. As stated before, walking in your purpose is not a solo act. As you take inventory of the people in your life, make sure you search within yourself with God's word and guidance to discover whether you are a liability to someone else's life, as well. Let us think about the option of free will that God grants us. Some of us pick and choose how we decide to live, not giving any true consideration to God's requirements of how His children should live on this Earth. We can unconsciously treat holiness as a buffet table—a little bit of this, a little bit of that, and none of this. Interestingly enough, we expect God to give His blessing on our "I'm doing me" approach to life. Living a free-for-all lifestyle may appear to be fun or even self-gratifying, but it is destructive to the nurturing needs of our purpose. In my younger years, I found myself questioning what I was taught as right because of demoralization in the world around me. Nowadays people choose what they want to obey from the Word of God; appearing to have no convictions about it. So, what is really the point of obeying? We are constantly bombarded with facts that overshadow God's truth. Yes, we are under His grace, but it does not mean we should abuse it. There are still consequences for sin which in turn becomes a liability to living in our purposes. Furthermore, it is not worth living outside of God's perfect will and short-changing the fulfillment of your purpose. Societal status is seemingly functional for today's lifestyle, but it is not by God's design. Sadly, we have learned to function in dysfunction and declared it to be the normal way of life. If you function in dysfunction, you are bound for destruction. The very moment we become comfortable with living as the world we are living a dysfunctional life. It is written in **Romans 12:2 New Living Translation,** *"Don't copy the behavior and customs of this world, but let God transform you into a new person by changing the way you think. Then you will learn to know God's will for you, which is good, acceptable, and perfect."* I would go out on a limb and say that many of us fail to fully submit our lives unto an obedient lifestyle because we haven't truly grasped the magnitude of our purpose or the sheer magnitude of our purpose actually scares us. Let me unpack that latter statement of fearing the great size of our purpose. When fear of inadequacy is present, we tend to act in a rebellious manner because we identify with our shortcomings rather than our power in God to be great. I know this because that was me; better yet, I am still overcoming remnants of this fear of being successful and the responsibility needed to stay at that level. If you casually continue to allow the conniving tactics of the enemy to rob you of living in your purpose, you will settle because of a "less-than" mindset. When we know who we are and Whose we are, we are more inclined to walk, talk, and act as such.

Your loyalty should be to your God-given purpose and His will for your life; not liabilities (people and/or a derailing lifestyle). Stop making single-game attendees into season ticket holders in your game of life; not everyone needs to be a part of all four quarters of it. Taking regular "circle checks" are healthy. Know that there is peace in your release.

Whatever liability you are holding onto that is against God's divine and perfect will for your life be it people or negative thinking, let it go! It will eventually create undo pressure and disrupt your overall wellbeing. Liabilities are like luggage; the more you have the heavier the load. Leave the liabilities behind!

**Daily Declaration**
"Let me hear of Your unfailing love each morning, for I am trusting You. Show me where to walk, for I give myself to You."

**Prayer**
Heavenly Father, grant me the wisdom to do what is right in your sight and live a life that is pleasing to You. You are Elohim Kedoshim,

the Holy God, and You desire for me to be holy before You. Forgive me for actions and speech that mirrors the world's way. Help me to fully let go of any connections with others that are liabilities to my purpose. I declare and decree that I am no longer entangled by the snares of the enemy that showed up in the form of relationships of any kind. I forego any ideologies that tried to derail my purpose. Send people that are for my journey; ones that will positively pour into me and me into them. In this season I pray you bring people into my life who will love me pass what I can do for them. Renew my mind, oh Lord, that I may have the mind of Christ. I surrender my "yes" to you now; forsaking any personal agendas that are outside Your will for me. Yield my heart to Your heart Father. Let Your truths invade every decision, every emotion, and every thought I have each day. I thank You for it now. This is my prayer in Jesus' name. Amen.

Today's song selection
"Yield My Heart" - Kim Walker-Smith

**Moment of Reflection**
1. What am I grateful to God for today?
2. How did I "Live in It" for my purpose today?
3. What did today's chapter reveal to me?
4. Did I allow God to be in control or did I allow myself to be my own God today? How did I or how did I not surrender control?

DAY 5

# I Said Amen... Now What?!

*"But blessed are those who trust in the Lord and have made the Lord their hope and confidence. They are like trees planted along a riverbank, with roots that reach deep into the water. Such trees are not bothered by the heat or worried by long months of drought. Their leaves stay green, and they never stop producing fruit."*
*Jeremiah 17:7-8 NLT*

Being connected to the right source is crucial. The right source will fuel you, guide you, and keep you for the journey. You can be connected to the right source, yet still not be fully charged. I recently had my cell phone charging in the wall unit. My cell phone was plugged in, but I noticed that I had to wiggle the wire to ensure it made the right connection to receive power. One night I plugged in my phone to charge right before bedtime. I heard the ding-noise it makes when it is connected, but I never looked at the screen to see whether the charge symbol appeared on the screen. I simply relied on what I heard to determine that my cell phone was charging. When I woke up the next morning, I saw that my cell phone did not charge at all. Yes, it was plugged in correctly, but it had less than twenty percent charge. As it is with us, we can be connected to the right source (God), but not extracting the power from the source to be fully effective in our purpose. The monotony of a routine tends to cause us to lose the zeal of pursuing our purpose; especially when we are in the trenches of going through the process. As with my cell phone, I simply relied on what I was used to hearing when it indicated it was being charged, but never took the time to make sure the connection was stable. Often when God gives us a word and we initially say, "Amen" in agreement we are pumped and ready to conquer the world. As time passes, our hope can begin to wane because of the lack of physical evidence of anything changing. After our "amen" comes the faith walk, where the rubber meets the road in our Christian journey. *Jeremiah 17:7 starts by saying that a person is blessed when he/she trusts in the Lord and his/her hope and confidence is in Him.* If we were going to unpack that sentence, we would see three operative words: trust, hope, and confidence. When I first thought about this verse, I questioned why trust was not the only thing needed to bring about the blessings referenced. If you look at verse 8 of the same chapter of Jeremiah, you will see the characteristic of someone whose trust, hope and confidence are in the Lord. Trusting God is the bedrock (foundation of your faith), but what makes it strong is when you make God your hope and confidence. This means not only do we trust God because of His character, but we are fully committed to resting our expectations and reliance solely on God's leading.

When we say amen, we are making a declaration of agreement. It is a declaration of resting in what God has spoken. One day I was getting ready for work and I asked God, "Lord, what does it mean to rest in You, Lord? I mean, really...what does rest in You mean for me?" At that point in time I knew God called me to a season of rest, but I knew it was not simply taking more daily naps type of rest. I did not know that I was about to enter a season of rapid (gut-wrenching) transition which could have wreak havoc on my hope. Experiencing the transition was one thing, but simultaneously having to yet again wait on God to move on major things in my life tested my hope in God, life, and people like no other! What I have learned in the process was not to sacrifice the good fruit that comes from waiting on God. Resting in the process of our purposes will allow God's perfect work to manifest in our lives; keeping us from life's sloppy seconds so we can have our Father's BEST! Can I get an amen?!

Surrendering your promise that is connected to your purpose may be a part of your "after amen" process. As most sixteen-year old is, I wanted a car. On the morning of my sixteenth birthday I kept looking outside of my home window for my car. I talked to my parents about this car for months on end. To my disappointment, I never saw it parked outside. I was secretly thinking to myself, "How could my parents miss this simple request? I did not even ask for a brand-new car; it could have been a used one for all I cared." My mother asked what I was looking for and I replied that I was checking to see what the weather conditions were for the day. Since it was my big day, she allowed me to drive her car to school. I was so sad, but I resisted the urge to throw a pity party to ruin my monumental birthday and upcoming slumber party. After that day I stopped asking for the car - whether it was out of lost hope or just trusting the fact that my parents said they would get me a car. Back in the day we had this Christmas family tradition in which my maternal side of the family would go over to my grandparents' home in the morning, eat breakfast and then open some of our presents. Since we lived the furthest away, all my presents were always brought over to my grandparents' house for me to open on Christmas Day. The Christmas in the same year of my 16th birthday I got everything I asked for and then some; so, I was beyond content. After we all opened our presents, my uncles anxiously requested that I take the trash bags filled with gift wrappings outside. You got to be kidding me! Why would a young sixteen-year-old girl need to take the trash out when there were four capable strong men available to do the job?! After my mini rant of having to take the trash out, I opened the front door and saw this shiny candy-apple Honda vehicle sitting in the driveway. I was completely shocked because no one mentioned getting a new car. I turned back around to see my family all looking at me and filming my reaction to what would be my new car! I screamed. I cried. My parents did not forget! I just got it when I least expected it. When you say amen expect what comes after it to be on God's timing. Have an attitude of, "God said it. I believe it. I receive it. Next." This four-part stance of listening to what God said, believing what He said, receiving what He said, and then saying "next" solidifies your commitment to trust God's heart towards you. Saying next means you are not going to be dismayed or moved by trying to figure out God's logistics such as the who, what, when, why, where, or how. Our brain naturally searches for context clues in the presence of ambiguity. Quite frankly, there will be times of uncertainty, but it does not negate the promises of God.

**Daily Declaration**
"Let me hear of Your unfailing love each morning, for I am trusting You. Show me where to walk, for I give myself to You."

**Prayer**
Gracious Father, continue to order my steps and grant me wisdom. I surrender my 'yes' to You; letting go of my expectations of how I think things should or should not go by simply resting in You. My expectations are in You. I declare You are God of my life, El Hayyay, and that You are sovereign. I know that after I say, "amen" the journey begins. Though the journey may not be devoid of trials, I know that I ultimately have the victory and everything that I shall place my hands upon shall prosper. Come Holy Spirit; I welcome You in. Father align my heart to Your heart. My hope and my confidence are in You. I will not waver in my faith and I will find solace in Your divine written and spoken Word. I thank You for never leaving me nor forsaking me. It is in Your precious son's name, Jesus, I pray. Amen.

**Today's song selection**
"Trust in You" - Lauren Daigle

Moment of Reflection:
1. What am I grateful to God for today?
2. How did I "Live in It" for my purpose today?
3. What did today's chapter reveal to me?
4. Did I allow God to be in control or did I allow myself to be my own God today? How did I or how did I not surrender control?

Let me hear of Your **unfailing** ♡ love each morning, for I am *trusting You.* Show me where to walk, for I give myself to *You.*

PSALM 143:8 NLT

DAY 6

# God Secured the Bag—YOU!

*"But you are not like that, for you are a chosen people. You are royal priests, a holy nation, God's very own possession. As a result, you can show others the goodness of God, for he called you out of the darkness into his wonderful light."*
1 Peter 2:9

The price of being chosen by God is the highest call anyone can answer. Walking the chosen path may present seasons of solitude from certain people because they may be a distraction to what God desires for you to do. Be vigilant to your inner circle of friends. Your destiny fulfillment is contingent to your connections. Check the season in which you are in and pray for clarity on whether if those you claim to be friends are meant to be attached to you for the journey. Everyone that may enter your life may not need to be a part of all four quarters of it.

When you are chosen you are set apart. Being God's chosen does not exempt anyone from experiencing trials contrary to popular belief. Yet, God reassures us that He sent His son who came to redeem us (*John 16:33 NLT "I have told you all this so that you may have peace in me. Here on earth you will have many trials and sorrows. But take heart because I have overcome the world."*). It is in this redemption we discover that although we may have trials our trials do not have us. There will be days you question whether your divine purpose is really for you because of the internal and external pressures you are experiencing. Take heart and know that God is with you; this is just the refining process. You are empowered to press through. Look in your mirror and say with great emphasis, "I am God's chosen, and my pathway is victorious!"

Being chosen means you are constantly on the Potter's wheel being molded into the vessel God has called you to be. Such as the clay on a potter's wheel, impurities must be removed in order to become the intended masterpiece. One morning I am getting ready for work and I just felt myself getting ready to cry out, "Why! Seriously God...why am I facing so much opposition?" But before I could even formulate the words I heard in my heart, "The pain you feel now is because I need you to be prepared to nurture the leaders of this nation that I am birthing through your womb." Do you realize that your chosen status is not about you? It is about what He is birthing through you for the advancement of His Kingdom. For this reason, you should choose to be submitted to the process.

Be encouraged knowing that the chosen life means a life covered with the powerful blood of Jesus, one of abundance with God's favor and blessings, and victory in every area of your life. It is an honor to be chosen by God—m*any are called, but few are chosen (Matthew 22:14)*. When God chose you, He secured the bag!

**Daily Declaration**

"Let me hear of Your unfailing love each morning, for I am trusting You. Show me where to walk, for I give myself to You."

**Prayer**

God, I want to endure like Jesus. Help me to get a vision for the joy of obtaining the prize that awaits me so that I can endure whatever trial comes my way. For I am Your chosen vessel. Jehovah Jireh: Lord You are my Provider. The One Who will provide a way through the opposition that I may face during the process. According to Isaiah 54:2, enlarge the place of my tent, and let them stretch out the curtains of my dwellings; do not spare; lengthen my cords, and strengthen my stakes oh Lord according to Your written word! Thank You that You have chosen me as Your heir to Your kingdom, that I am a child of the Most High King and by virtue of my relationship with You through Your son Jesus Christ, I inherit all of the spiritual blessings that You have for me in Your kingdom. Thank you for your abundant favor. I pray this in confidence in You; knowing that the price of being chosen may be high, but it is well worth it. Thank You Father. In Jesus' name. Amen.

**Today's song selection**
"Worth" - Anthony Brown and Group TherAPy

**Moment of Reflection**
1. What am I grateful to God for today?
2. How did I "Live in It" for my purpose today?

3. What did today's chapter reveal to me?
4. Did I allow God to be in control or did I allow myself to be my own God today? How did I or how did I not surrender control?

DAY 7

# Peace In the Midst of Chaos

*"But when I am afraid, I will put my trust in You."*
*Psalm 56:3 NLT*

There is no price tag that we can put on having peace. Peace is priceless. Remember the Lord Great and Awesome—God worked your past challenges out for the purpose so when you got to your challenges of today you can look back and know He has your today.

During a recent flight from Houston, TX to Washington, DC I experienced some of the worst turbulence ever in my 20 plus years of flying. While we were taxied at the gate before takeoff, the pilot came on the intercom and stated that it would be bumpy at first as we ascend to flying altitude. He said once we leveled off it would then be a smooth flight into DC. The mighty force of the wind jolted the aircraft ferociously as if it were a toy plane. It literally felt like we were about to drop from the sky. I was resting my eyes, but I could feel my grip get tighter around the armrest. As I began to pray, I replayed what the pilot initially said about being bumpy as we ascended to the flying altitude. Though the shaking of the plane was very unpleasant and felt like eternity, I had the assurance that it would soon end at flying altitude.

Just as in your own life, as you begin to elevate in your purpose you will experience turbulence (opposition, misfortune, setbacks, and so on). Being a saved, Holy Ghost-filled Christian does not exempt you from the trials of life. Matter of fact prepare even more for the rough patches just because you are a chosen vessel of God. The enemy is stark mad and will do everything in his limited power to destroy your destiny. Just as the pilot assured us that the turbulence would not last, so is God as He reminds us of what is in His written word, "Trouble do not last always..."

You may experience anxiety during chaotic moments which opens the door to worrying. The act of worrying is a sin because it is meditating (pondering heavily) on the thoughts created by satan, (the accuser/liar/adversary), rather than on what God said. God's written word blatantly states you can find peace in chaos because God is covering you as a shield. Our Abba Father grants us peace that surpasses all understanding. The pressure you feel is not to penalize you, but it is to propel you into your purpose. Keep your perspective on your purpose and not on the pain. Keep your focus on God's presence and not the pressure. Make a conscious effort to live in a mental and heart space of "this too shall pass."

Just as past chaotic situations that came into your life, it will all die because God is faithful to His word and will make a way. It is in God's written word in R*omans 5:1-5 NLT, "Therefore, since we have been made right in God's sight by faith, we have peace with God because of what Jesus Christ our Lord has done for us.* Because of our faith, Christ has brought us into this place of undeserved privilege where we now stand, and we confidently and joyfully look forward to sharing God's glory. We can rejoice, too, when we run into problems and trials, for we know that they help us develop endurance. And endurance develops strength of character, and character strengthens our confident hope of salvation. And this hope will not lead to disappointment. For we know how dearly God loves us, because he has given us the Holy Spirit to fill our hearts with his love." The greater the attack on your life is the greater the anointing on your purpose. Remember there is no failure in God; Jesus died to bless you! You are a failed-proof success story—say it, believe it, walk it.

**Daily Declaration**
"Let me hear of Your unfailing love each morning, for I am trusting You. Show me where to walk, for I give myself to You."

**Prayer**
Lord, Father, God You are my peace. You are my strength. Jehovah Shammah, the Lord that is there for me. Your word says that You will never leave nor forsake me. Grant me peace that surpasses all understanding in the chaotic moments of life. I will not be derailed by uncomfortable situations that feel like a lifetime sentence. Each

challenge will be an opportunity to elevate in the promises You already made available for me. For I know that trouble do not last always. I am filled with the Holy Spirit which comforts me. I dispatch my Heavenly angels to encompass around me as a shield - a mighty force to fight against any satanic plot to derail me of my purpose-path. Merciful Father grant me divine wisdom to have victory over every area of my life. You are my Father, Lord, and Savior. Thank You for loving me, God. I praise You. In Jesus' name. Amen.

Today's song selection
"Made A Way" - Travis Greene

**Moment of Reflection**
1. What am I grateful to God for today?
2. How did I "Live in It" for my purpose today?
3. What did today's chapter reveal to me?
4. Did I allow God to be in control or did I allow myself to be my own God today? How did I or how did I not surrender control?

DAY 8

# Take Your Hands Out of the Cookie Jar

*"Call to Me, and I will answer you, and show you great and mighty things, which you do not know."*
*Jeremiah 33:3*

Many years ago God began to deal with me about control. I was the kind of person that needed to know how everything was going to play out, who all will be involved, and what the time frame would be to make it happen. Having to know "how" was the limitation I placed on my level of trust in God. The reason for all of this "in the know" disposition was because I wanted to have as much access as possible to make any necessary changes I deemed critical for my success; especially if Plan A (God's plan) looked like it was failing. It was revealed to me that I suffered from a form of pride which manifested itself in wanting to control the situation on my terms; not fully relying on God. Unfortunately, the pride that I used to suffer from had a sibling tagging along with it—fear. Pride coupled with fear are the dynamic duo destructing the fulfillment of purposes. When I started putting my hands into the situation things would fall apart, but I would somehow blame God.

The need to have all the answers can trip us up along the journey of purpose. This is a form of control because knowledge gives a sense of security and power. Often when God is intentionally silent our anxiety level rises in search of an answer. This anxiety leads to the notion that we must "do something" to make things happen favorably. I coined this effect the "Cookie Jar Syndrome." You see, too many hands in the cookie jar causes cross-contamination; what was once sweet and good is now spoiled because of too many manipulative touches compromising the cookies' freshness. This is what God gave me to visually understand the importance of me taking my hands-off things that are already in His hands to do. When you start to put your hands into the situation without consulting God, you become your own god. It is in these moments you need to remember that faith looks forward. If everything were tangible and visible it would not require faith. It would not require belief in God's deity. In Hebrews 11:6 it reads, *"And it is impossible to please God without faith."* Our first mission is to please God. You cannot allow yourself to get so caught up in the current bleak situation that you stop striving in faith to take hold of the promise set before you. When you go through the process of fulfilling your purpose, get a "forward-focus perspective". This is a "no-matter-what-happens" posture you take to avoid putting your hands in the cookie jar! Do not let what is behind you make you miss what is ahead of you! What would happen if you drove your vehicle only looking in the rear-view mirror? Shall we say a major accident? The rear-view mirror is a safety device used to help you, the driver, increase your awareness with a quick glance. The same goes as it relates to those things which are behind you from your past. Our hindsight should only give us insight for our present to have foresight to our future.

At the beginning of 2016, God showed me His mathematical equation to obtain His miracles. He said Faith + Obedience = Miracles. It is not by the works of our hands or our intellect to stir up God's miraculous. Faith in things that embodies the essence of God coupled with obedience to His commands both create the atmosphere to birth His miracles! When you have experienced setbacks and disappointments, it can be challenging to walk out this faith path without reverting to controlling tactics to protect your heart from expectation woes. Unmet expectations can create a distorted view of God's heart towards you. Have you sat down and reflected on why you stopped expecting greater from God? If you were to be honest with yourself, the source of your disappointment is because God did not do what you wanted Him to do in the way you wanted (expected) Him to do it. God will never let you live a life that makes Him unnecessary. I believe when you begin to increase your expectations of God you become more aligned to the abundance; He already has for you. You just needed to be in the posture to receive it all.

Timing is everything. We may not understand all of God's moves, but we understand His motives. He does all that He does because of His unconditional love for us. Anointing and appointing collide to bring about the full manifestation of God through your purpose.

As today's scripture says, call on God for He is ready to answer and show you great and mighty things that surpasses your imagination. Release control unto Him and keep a ready heart of expectancy. Yes, you will have your moments when you just want to break free from what seems like chains holding you back from what you desire to do. Proceed with caution though because a temporal moment can lead to permanent memories to yet hurdle over.

**Daily Declaration**
"Let me hear of Your unfailing love each morning, for I am trusting You. Show me where to walk, for I give myself to You."

**Prayer**
Father, I admit today that I have wrongfully tried to take control over things in my life that I needed to surrender over to You. Forgive me for the worry, doubt, fear, anxiety, anger and even lack of love that is in my heart at times and cleanse me in Your holiness. Oh God Your Son is El Roi the strong One Who sees me. You see past what my mere mortal eyes can see and do far more than what I can do in my own strength. I take my hands out of the cookie jar God, and let You take the reins. This battle is not mine, but it is Yours. Lord, grant me the wisdom and the ability to press through the restriction I am experiencing into a time of acceleration in my purpose. Let not my mind be bombarded with unsettling thoughts

that will try to get me to make impulsive decisions on my own that was not in Your perfect will. I will follow Your lead. In Jesus' holy and matchless name. Amen.

Today's song selection
"The Anthem" - Todd Dulaney

**Moment of Reflection**
1. What am I grateful to God for today?
2. How did I "Live in It" for my purpose today?
3. What did today's chapter reveal to me?
4. Did I allow God to be in control or did I allow myself to be my own God today? How did I or how did I not surrender control?

DAY 9

# The Weight of Waiting

*"We were given this hope when we were saved. (If we already have something, we do not need to hope for it. But if we look forward to something we do not yet have, we must wait patiently and confidently.)".*
*Romans 8:24-25 NLT*

When you are anxiously waiting for something great to manifest, it can often feel like a heavy weight on your heart. I have discovered that our life challenges are permitted. They are sifted through the hand of God specifically to build us up to be prepared for what is yet to come in our lives. God is too strategic to randomly allow anything in your life that is not for your elevation. So, if God permitted it then it will build the faith muscle you need whether for your life specifically or for the testimony you will share to help somebody along the way. The weight of waiting can be heavy, frustrating, and discouraging. It is in the wait the devil will pester you with negative thoughts to try to make you question God's plans, love, and character altogether. If you are wavering in your faith during waiting periods, your focus will be on the magnitude of the situation instead of the magnificence of the Savior. What do you do in the waiting period? It is simple - stay before God's face by worshipping unto Him, reading and studying His written word, and speaking life only! Great, the steps are simple to follow. However, the challenge arises is in the process of following steps as you wait. It requires God's strength and laser focus. But above all else, guarding your heart from the entanglements set before you by the enemy is critical. The waiting season is to build your trust relationship with the Father while alleviating fear that will try to overshadow your faith. This journey begins with faith and ends with hope. This kind of hope is developed in spite challenging seasons of your life because it is not based on circumstances or people.

As it relates to your purpose, it is vital that you know the season that God placed you in - is it harvest season, planting season, pruning season, gleaning season, or etcetera? Many times, we are misaligned because we are trying to collect our harvest in the winter seasons of our lives.

"The only thing harder than waiting on God is wishing you had." This was a statement made by Pastor Steven Furtick of Elevation Church in Charlotte, North Carolina. The one place you do not want to be is on the other side of your impatience. The wait may be weighty, but it brings the strength to sustain the blessing of your purpose. Commit to the flow of the process. Ask yourself, "What is my attitude like during the wait?" You may have heard the phrase that your attitude determines your aptitude. This is so true.

Your attitude sets the tone for your season of waiting; it is the key ingredient to help you find pleasure in the process. Think about it from this standpoint: a heavy wait vs. an expectant wait. A heavy wait is an emotional rollercoaster because of the circumstances and the pressure that comes in the process. It feels heavy because the weight of the blessing and your focus which is on the problem. An expectant wait is a "despite how I may feel"/an "oh well" stance *despite* the circumstances and the pressure that comes in the process. It feels expectant because the hopefulness of what is to come and your focus which is on the purpose of the problem at hand.

It is a "not my will, but Your will be done" perspective/attitude that will yield your heart to trust God's peace and love. Trust God when you cannot trace Him; trust Him past your emotions that try to compare God to the shortcomings of people in your past who failed you.

**Daily Declaration**
"Let me hear of Your unfailing love each morning, for I am trusting You. Show me where to walk, for I give myself to You."

**Prayer**
My Lord, my Father, and my God; thank You for an abundant life far beyond what I could ever imagine. You are Jehovah Uzi, my Strength. I will not shrink back in my walk with You because of the weight of waiting. I will hold on tightly to Your unchanging hand and stand on Your unadulterated word for guidance and strength. I want to live a life demonstrating Your power God. Help me to

live a life that is dependent on Your grace and power to achieve things I never thought possible through my life. God Your word says that You are for me. So, who can be against me? I will humble myself as I wait for the manifestation of the promises connected to my purpose. All these things I declare, and decree done in Jesus' name. Amen.

Today's Song Selection
"Don't Mind Waiting"- Juanita Bynum

**Moment of Reflection**
1. What am I grateful to God for today?
2. How did I "Live in It" for my purpose today?
3. What did today's chapter reveal to me?
4. Did I allow God to be in control or did I allow myself to be my own God today? How did I or how did I not surrender control?

DAY 10

# Fill Your Tank

*"For He satisfies the thirsty and fills the hungry with good things."*
*Psalm 107:9 NLT*

God has drawn me to things that are centered on seeking His face and His presence. According to Matthew 6:33 we are called to seek the Kingdom of God above all else, and live righteously, and He will give you everything you need. This scripture reminds us that in His presence there is true fullness of joy. When I think of being in God's presence, I think back to my first personal encounter with the Holy Spirit. It was the most surreal moment that was so unexplainably peaceful. I cried buckets of tears as I laid in a fetal position on the cold cement-made church floor. I heard one of my prayer partners talking to me. My eyes were closed tightly, but my ears were totally alert. Honestly, I really did not hear her voice.

The melodic voice I heard shared things about my ancestors... my purpose...my future. I wanted to lay there in that moment. That moment in God's presence was indescribable.

When I got my first car my parents harped about keeping a full tank of gas in it. My mother does not even like to drive on a half tank of gas. They emphasized the importance of keeping my gas tank on full to increase the longevity of my vehicle, as well as, eliminate harmful sediments from entering into my fuel filter. In addition to this advice, they said, "beware of bad gas". Sounds funny, right?! Basically, what they were letting me know was that not all gas quality is created equal; the lower quality grade gas typically lacks the extra additives used to protect the engine. I believe this is the same notion as it relates to our daily interactions with God. **The fuel for your purpose comes from being in God's presence; receiving strength and restoration to fulfill your purpose through the good fight of faith.** We are fueled by our proximity to the Father. It is in this closeness we are able to fortify our faith to withstand the attacks of the devil. Our God is drawing us back to an intimate place to quiet our thoughts so that He may fill our minds with divine strategies and witty inventions. When we run low on our interactions with our Heavenly Father, we then run low on our beliefs in our identity we are in Him. God states that we are very precious, chosen, holy vessels, beloved children belonging to Him. Knowing this about ourselves is essential to our spiritual core. Taking a seat with the Father helps us to uproot the fears and the doubts (the "bad gas") that got wedged in our hearts from not spending face-to-faith time with Him. He is saying, "All you have need of is in My word; draw nigh unto Me."

God is looking for the "here I am's"; these are His children whose hearts and actions that say, "Here I am Lord." We have gotten to a place where we are so wrapped up in personal agendas - not to exclude ministry agendas—in which we have forgotten to just be in God's presence. We should be a willing vessel crying out: *Here I Am Lord!* Sometimes, that "here I am" is an opportunity to just rest in His presence; not necessarily receiving instructions on what to do next. Better yet, it is an opportunity to get a fresh anointing to fill our tanks for the unknowns that lie ahead that will require great faith. Sit and relax at His feet, withholding nothing. There are times He just wants us to be still and hear His heartbeat towards you.

As a kid, when it was God and me time, I would close my eyes and imagine sitting in His great big lap with my knees tucked to my chest and my head nestled right below His left chest. I would envision Him playing with my hair and saying, "Hey My Lanna." Sometimes neither one of us would talk which was perfectly okay with me. It was how I would center myself before I even knew what that meant. It was my innocent way of filling my spiritual tank. It is that childlike innocence God is calling us to to lean in His direction to fill us with the good things He has for us.

If you would seek God as if you were desperate, then you would not be desperate for the things of this world that will leave you empty. Fill your tank up by being in God's presence daily. Running on empty spiritually keeps you from experiencing the fullness of your purpose.

**Daily Declaration**

"Let me hear of Your unfailing love each morning, for I am trusting You. Show me where to walk, for I give myself to You."

**Prayer**

My Lord, my Savior, my Provider, and my Shield. I come to You thanking You for the promises You have given me. Forgive me for trying to figure out when and the how it is going to be manifested in my life. Kings see You and bow down. I pray that I will live each moment in that same spirit of honor and humility before You God. For You know what steps I should take and how to guide me. Amen

**Today's Song Selection**

"Fill Me Up" - Casey J

**Moment of Reflection**

1. What am I grateful to God for today?
2. How did I "Live in It" for my purpose today?
3. What did today's chapter reveal to me?
4. Did I allow God to be in control or did I allow myself to be my own God today? How did I or how did I not surrender control?

DAY 11

# When Delay Looks Like No—Endure Patiently

*"God blesses those who patiently endure testing and temptation". Afterward they will receive the crown of life that God has promised to those who love him. And remember when you are being tempted, do not say, "God is tempting me." God is never tempted to do wrong, and he never tempts anyone else. Temptation comes from our own desires, which entice us and drag us away. These desires give birth to sinful actions. And when sin can grow, it gives birth to death. So, do not be misled, my dear brothers and sisters. Whatever is good and perfect is a gift coming down to us from God our Father, who created all the lights in the heavens. He never changes or casts a shifting shadow. He chose to give birth to us by giving us his true word. And we, out of all creation, became his prized possession."*

*James 1:12-18 NLT*

The pain of process provokes you to pray and praise to promote you and make you operate in His power that is already in you. The Purpose Process: Pray - Praise - Promotion - Power. When God gives us a word about our promised purpose, there is not a Heavenly manual that drops down from the sky. Matter of fact, the process is generally not disclosed by God because He is using the process to build our trust and faith in Him. In my trust walk with God, the following two statements have kept me pursuing my purpose and enduring the process: "your process is your process" and "what you do not see is more real than what you do see". Basically, you cannot compare your purpose journey to anyone else's or allow your physical sight of your current circumstances to disrupt your spiritual sight of what God promised you. God has given you the grace to run your own race. It seems like a delay, but let it play. This means let the process play out as God intended by staying the course.

    A friend of mine was driving in the rain and he unknowingly made a profound comment while navigating through the downpour, "It's funny how you can't see, but you can see." That is how it is when going through the process and you approach a patch of rain called delay; making your expectation of fulfilling your purpose seem like God is saying, "No." A delay is an opportunity for bestowing greater glory unto God and is the breathing ground for divine miracles.

    It is written in *Psalm 37:34* that when we wait on the Lord and keep His way (obey His instructions to stay the course) He will exalt us to inherit the land. In the moments of perceived delay, it is important to surround yourself with people who can provide wise counsel, pray throughout the day *every day*, and read all you can about the Lord. We must evaluate our circle. The reason for this is because it is in this moment the enemy will play with your mind to make you question if God is really on your side or if what you heard Him say was valid. This is when your endurance is like a muscle in your body. For a muscle to build up there is a tearing that first takes place within the muscle; followed by soreness. Just like muscles, there are situations that may arise in your life that will break you and stretch you. In this breaking and stretching your faith is building as your expectation for God to show up grows.

Waiting is not a reflection of who you are nor Whose you are. Waiting is the training period for you to get clarity on your identity so that you can make wise decision from a settled state of mind. Waiting is the pruning period in which God uses to revive our relationship with God and breakup with our desire to get the manifestation of what God promised in your own way.

**Daily Declaration**
"Let me hear of Your unfailing love each morning, for I am trusting You. Show me where to walk, for I give myself to You."

**Prayer:**
Gracious Father in Heaven, I thank You for this day. Help me to endure patiently like Jesus and to have Your greater perspective as I wait on You to manifest the promised purpose of my life. God, I do not want to be lost in the pursuit of what You already have for me. Forgive me if I have lost my mind or way in anxiety trying to rush Your hands to give me what I want outside of its time. El Bethel, The God of the house of God, abide in me. Grant me the **discernment to know how to reflect you well.** I give You my whole heart, mind, and soul so that I will be strengthen in my faith in You. I trust You far beyond what my physical eyes can see, and my ever-changing emotions may feel. It is in Your Son's precious name, Jesus Christ, that I lay any weariness down. Amen.

Today's Song Selection

"You Are My Strength" - William Murphy

**Moment of Reflection**
1. What am I grateful to God for today?
2. How did I "Live in It" for my purpose today?
3. What did today's chapter reveal to me?
4. Did I allow God to be in control or did I allow myself to be my own God today? How did I or how did I not surrender control?

A DELAY is an OPPORTUNITY for bestowing GREATER GLORY unto GOD.

DAY 11

DAY 12

# Unauthorized Gap Fillers

*"But when you ask him, be sure that your faith is in God alone. Do not waver, for a person with divided loyalty is as unsettled as a wave of the sea that is blown and tossed by the wind."*
*James 1:6 NLT*

Y ou cannot shortcut God's plans. This means you need not judge living with purpose based upon how you feel; or make life-altering decisions based upon your feelings. How you feel is rooted in your emotions (facts filtered through your ears and eyes) mixed with your past experiences then coined as reality posing to be truth. Feelings, as we know it, are fickle. They are temporal state of emotions. The only truth comes from God's written and spoken word. The devil presents facts as an illusion of truth because they are tangible current happenings that can easily derail your purpose if you give much thought to them. This is when unauthorized gap fillers are introduced into your life to fill the void of the unknown that is presented in a season of waiting on the divine appointment. The goal of the enemy is to distract you; take your focus off what God instructed you to do. Fear often (if not *all* the time) is what the enemy uses to distract us, causing derailment to the future. Distractions are the silent killers of purpose. Think of it like this, our body yearns for food; the elements required to eliminating hunger. Our body needs nutrients to preserve optimal functionality. We can eat practically anything regardless of nutritional value to solve our hunger. `The problem is that everything we eat may not be healthy for our bodies' wealth. In the same school of thought, we may yearn for a desire of our hearts and unintentionally operate in disobedience to God's will to fulfill what our hearts want. Unfortunately, the fear of God not answering our desire the way in which we want it when we want it leads us to fill the emptiness with unfruitful relationships, occupations, purchases, etc. We cannot allow fear to fill a void that only God's love can do.

As you are trailblazing your purpose, sometimes you will experience burnout. When that starts to happen, check your source. Is your source God or you? Are you doing things in God's strength or in yours? Is God your burden-bearer or are you your own burden-bearer? All these questions are good checkpoint questions to ask yourself and reflect upon when you feel the fatigue of going through the process of purpose. Note that it is in those vulnerable times that true resting in God and in your physical body are imperative. The devil will attack your mind and heart towards your purpose in moments of weariness. He will present you with all the facts which on the outside look like you heard incorrectly from

Lord, made a wrong decision, cannot win, and/or etc. Yes, it may be a fact you are experiencing an insurmountable opposition right now in which you cannot control. But the truth is God said that He would never leave nor forsake you; He is willing and able to take full control of the situation if you let Him. The scheme of the devil is to fill the holes in your thoughts with rerun episodes of your failed or hurtful experiences as if they were new happenings. This is how the enemy leverages weariness to attack your progression of operating in your purpose by. As a human race, we do not like gaps. We are always trying to fill it with something because gaps are viewed as a deficiency. What if we shift our perspective about these seemingly flawed holes in our lives? What if we view them as reflective pauses alerting us that it is time to fast and pray to obtain wisdom and insight to grow in our walks with God? The gaps are indicative to the need for spiritual intimacy with our Creator. *Pursuing the heart of the Father automatically gives us the hand of the Father (Matthew 6:33). Ephesians 1:17 states that we should ask our glorious Father to give us spiritual wisdom and insight to increase our knowledge of Him.* Our gaps remind us of how far we have come and how much we need God to grow in us.

**Daily Declaration**
"Let me hear of Your unfailing love each morning, for I am trusting You. Show me where to walk, for I give myself to You."

**Prayer**
Abba Father, I praise You for you are faithful, loving and kind towards me. Forgive me for positioning people and things

in unauthorized places my life. Forgive me for using them to resolve what needed to come from You. Elohei Chasdi, you are my stronghold and the God who shows me loving kindness. I confess that I do not always look to You as my stronghold, but rather attempt to solve my problems on my own. Forgive me for neglecting to make You the focal point when I am facing various trials or heartache. For Your faithfulness, kindness, and goodness are my true comfort. I declare I will not grow weary in well doing. In the appointed time I will reap my harvest because I did not give up. I pray for Your guidance and strength to position myself in the flow of Your Spirit in order to accomplish much more with less effort. Fill me up God; have all of me. I pray this in Your matchless Son Jesus's name. Amen.

**Today's Song Selection**
"Your Destiny" - Kevan LeVar

**Moment of Reflection**
1. What am I grateful to God for today?
2. How did I "Live in It" for my purpose today?
3. What did today's chapter reveal to me?
4. Did I allow God to be in control or did I allow myself to be my own God today? How did I or how did I not surrender control?

DAY 13

# Be. Humble.

*"Humble yourselves before the Lord, and he will lift you up in honor."*
*James 4:10 NLT*

There is a catchy song by a Hip Hop Artist named Kendrick Lamar entitled, "Humble". The chorus repeatedly states for the person to be humble. Humility is such a key characteristic to the activation of your purpose. As you are flowing in your calling it is not uncommon to desire validation from others; to feel significant from their approval. True significance comes from fulfilling the God-given purpose for which you were made. In this social media "look at me" age influencers have created a platform for themselves by becoming popular. This popularity and clout do not necessarily mean the influencer has the academic credentials to be considered a legit subject matter expert. What the influencer has is their presence. Only thing is, those who create a name for themselves God thought of you before He presented you. There is nothing outside of God's will for you to do.

Fulfilling your purpose is not for you to find contentment in the possessions it may bring or the perceivable clout, but instead it is to foster a relationship with God in the process that brings unwavering joy and contentment. Consider Paul when he spoke to the church of Philippi, the first congregation of Europe, and said, "I have learned to be content whatever the circumstances. I know what it is to be in need, and I know what it is to have plenty. *I have learned the secret of being content in any and every situation, whether well fed or hungry, whether living in plenty or in want.*" —Philippians 4:11-12

God is strategically developing your character in manner that is pure of heart and free of any sediments of destructive behavior. He does this for you to take hold of the mantle as the righteousness of Christ without making the mantle an idol. The platform set before is not to be worshipped hence the character transformation that takes place along the journey to and in your purpose. Just because someone may purchase a luxury car it does not always mean they have the continued cash flow to maintain ownership of that car. Basically, God will not allow you to be way over your head and unprepared for succeeding in your purpose. Every part of the process has a purpose. The process you go through is training ground for being a faithful steward of the purpose gave you. As you excel in your purpose it is not for you to get the big head and think it was all you that made you "arrive". When God gives you a gift, calling, and a purpose He is entrusting you with an expectation of taking this gift, calling, and purpose to perfect it, make it better and multiply it in order for you to give back to Him double. It is in the double return that can be an open door for haughty thinking and acting. Do you love the position more than you love the purpose? Is the door that God opened for you because of your obedience to walk in your purpose causing you to think more highly of yourself than you ought to? God takes to positions in your life. He either exalts you or He humbles you. Father God will not fight with you and your will. So, if you choose the path of puffing up yourself to boast, He will lovingly humble you. If you go in the direction of humility, God with a Father's pride will exalt you. God will entrust you with more when He can trust your modest character.

God did not create us to be islanders in isolation without the aid of others. We are relational beings just as our Father. With that being said, it is imperative that you are connected to an accountability partner that will stand in the gap with you when the journey gets rocky, will check-in with you on your progress, will hold you accountable to what God has placed in your hands to complete. Some may think that Do not let desperation lead you to deprivation. Thank God for the long route. *Psalm 119:71 MSG humble.* You are not to throw yourself a gloat party to have people solely praise you. Your win is to give God glory. What if the price you paid with your pain is the payment needed to pave the way for someone else? Everything you been through will not be wasted. Your hurtful experiences can be the pathway in which your children's children will not have to suffer such things as (just to name a few) poverty, abuse, or even poor education.

**Daily Declaration**

"Let me hear of Your unfailing love each morning, for I am trusting You. Show me where to walk, for I give myself to You."

**Prayer**

Gracious and merciful God, You alone are worthy to be praised. You are the mighty King. Thank You for being everything I need and more. I honor You because You are great; there is none like You. I ask for forgiveness for all the things I have done to grieve You. Jehovah Rohi, The Lord my Shepherd, order my steps in your way dear Lord so that I may remain humble before You. I desire to follow You wholeheartedly. I pray my heart remains joyful as I serve You with obedience to the call over my life. Father, continue to watch over me. I ask that You please strip me of all selfish intent and prideful demeanor that puts a wedge between our relationship. I realize that it is not about religion or religious acts, but it is about being one with You, Abba, as I operate in spirit and in truth. Thank You for loving me the way that You do. I give You praise. In Jesus' name. Amen.

**Today's Song Selection**
"Make Room" – Jonathan McReynolds

**Moment of Reflection**
1. What am I grateful to God for today?
2. How did I "Live in It" for my purpose today?
3. What did today's chapter reveal to me?

4. Did I allow God to be in control or did I allow myself to be my own God today? How did I or how did I not surrender control?

"Humble Yourselves before the Lord and He will lift you up in Honor."

JAMES 4:10 NLT

DAY 14

# Resurrected Vision: Dream Again

*"May the God of hope fill you with all joy and peace as you trust in him, so that you may overflow with hope by the power of the Holy Spirit."*
Romans 15:13 NLT

Destiny does not ask circumstances permission to continue. Despite how things are currently or may seem, your destiny/purpose still lives. Do not operate according to your circumstances, mistakes, and/or disappointments. Rise above it in faith. Faith in knowing that your destiny still has your name on it, and it *will* come to pass at God's appointed time! You must begin to dream again! I have this weekly routine on Sunday mornings to start my day by listening to different preachers on television as I get ready for church. This one Sunday I was listening to Dr. Pierre Bennett of God's Luv International Ministries Church in Silver Spring, MD. He preached a message entitled, "This Time Tomorrow". As I was absorbing what he was saying, I looked up at the television screen and saw, "Still to Come" in the lower left corner. Now, I know that statement was referencing what was to come in the message after the short 30 second commercial break. However, that "still to come" message along with his sermon about not giving up during the periods that feel like defeat when you are doing what God called you to do, resonated so strongly within me. I believe it was God's unique way of reminding me that greater is still to come because the victory which I cannot see is more real than the opposition that I can see.

Dreaming is keeping the vision of your purpose at the forefront of your brain. Develop ways to nurture your dream because any living thing needs nutrients; without adequate nourishment it will die. Ever seen a dead person that is alive? Trust me you have. Just observe a person that has given up on a dream, cutting off the lifeline to their purpose. That my friend is what is referred to being a dead person living. I was getting ready for work one day and BAM—it hits me! The nature of my former job was sucking the life out of me because I was living in a shell of myself. As I expressed it to one of my accountability partners, my physical and mental exhaustion stemmed from the burden of merely existing at my 9 to 5 where I was forcing myself to operate outside of my purpose. It was like God asking me, "Are you agitated enough yet to do what I told you to do?!" I am certain a lot of us are scared to charter unfamiliar territory because of the magnitude of our dreams. Some may even fear how great they will be. Sounds crazy, right? I believe the presence of fear comes into play in this instance because some of us have never been exposed to success that produces great fortune in the form of increased revenue, recognition, or responsibility. We subconsciously worry if we have what it takes to maintain that level of greatness. No one ever really wants to be known as the "one hit wonder". Well, it is crazy. It is crazy to live a life that is not yours–a self-manufactured and presumed secure life that is below God's divinely ordained path for you. Having faith does not mean we have all the answers. It means we can grow through the journey and cope with the unanswered questions or undisclosed details.

We are connected to the ultimate Dreamer–God. So, if we are connected to the Son of the living God, the Dreamer, who plants seeds of dreams in us then that means our dreams are alive! Our dreams may be dormant, but they are never dead because God is alive! Do you know what the purpose of the agitator in the washing machine? The cylinder fixture in the center of the washing machine is known as the agitator. The agitator is designed to disrupt the fabric fibers of clothing items to remove the dirt and stain from them. I am sure if the clothes were given human personification, they would be frustrated and irritated to no end while being tossed around the washer all throughout the necessary cycles of the cleaning process. It is the same with us. God allows situations to arise in our lives to agitate–disrupt our scheduled plans – to rid us of the people, things, and ideologies that will prevent us from dreaming.

**Daily Declaration**
Let me hear of Your unfailing love each morning, for I am trusting You. Show me where to walk, for I give myself to You."

**Prayer**

Gracious and merciful Father, you are the ultimate dream Giver. You are El Shaddai, the Lord God Almighty. I honor You today by reflecting on what You have already spoken. I will not allow the time it has taken for the dream to come true to distance my walk with You. You are more real than the dream I await to come. I will exalt You oh Father. Be Lord in every area of my life as You are my joy and my peace. I praise Your Holy name and give You glory. I declare that all that I have need of and desire are already done. Reestablish my faith in You Abba. Revive my hope so my heart will freely dream once more. Grant me the wisdom on how to protect my peace as I wait on You. Thank You God for restoring my expectation in You. Eyes have not seen, nor ears have not heard all that You have planned for me. In Jesus' name. Amen.

**Today's Song Selection**
"Do It Again" - Elevation Worship

**Moment of Reflection**
1. What am I grateful to God for today?
2. How did I "Live in It" for my purpose today?
3. What did today's chapter reveal to me?
4. Did I allow God to be in control or did I allow myself to be my own God today? How did I or how did I not surrender control?

DAY 15

# Power of Now

*"For God says, "At just the right time, I heard you.*
*On the day of salvation, I helped you.*
*"Indeed, the "right time" is now. Today is the day of salvation."*
*2 Corinthians 6:2*

Yesterday was once now, and now will soon be tomorrow. When we chase after tomorrow, we are yearning for the gift of now. The power of the present is something that is often overlooked because of our tendency to live for tomorrow and not for today. Ever find yourself saying, "Tomorrow I will..." or "I cannot wait until tomorrow when..." When will we say, "Today, I will..." or "I cannot wait until today..."? The present is truly that—a *present*. The gift of today brings about God's mercies which are made new each day. Do not fall victim to a "should have/could have" debilitating cycle. There are millions of people that have allowed the passing of time to strangle their minds that were once filled with brilliant ideas needed to nurture their purpose. Now, they are walking around talking about "if I only knew then what I know now..." or "I wish I had ...". I once heard my former pastor say that the wealthiest place on Earth is the graveyard; meaning so many people die never fully expensing their gifts and talents to flourish in their respective purposes. Quite frankly it is a sad notion to think about.

Generally, it is not always a case of lack of awareness, but mainly a fixation on limited resources that keep us from not moving in the season of "now". In other words, if we only focus on what we think we need to fulfill our purpose; then more than likely we will not make any headway towards the manifestation of it. The adversary (the devil) will convolute our minds with thoughts of things we cannot control—the how is and the when's—so much so, it immobilizes our focus on only our inabilities rather than God's infinite abilities. Did you know that every time we fret about our limitations and worry about the results of a matter we basically put Jesus Christ back on the cross saying that His death was not powerful enough to handle the situation? Yikes! Jesus's death was enough the first time! Just like what you have inside of you is enough!

Do not keep putting off what can be down today for tomorrow; for tomorrow is not promised to us. God is making a mandate on many of us to move into what He has called us to do today. Each moment we delay we are deliberately rejecting His commands. Delayed obedience is still disobedience. The cost of delay is too high because whether you know it or not, there are lives connected to your "now" movement. Take myself for example; this devotional book was my baby I needed to birth out for the masses to read. Trust me it was a true labor of love to birth this baby. Every time I would delay in spending time with God and getting still to hear His voice for the book's content, I was holding up what you, the reader, needed for your purpose walk. Do I personally know all of you? No. But Abba Father does, and I was just a vessel He used to share His instructions.

I want to be clear on what God means when He expresses the power of now. Now as instructed by God is what I would call an urgent command with peace. You see, many times we are presented the opportunities or situations that require an immediate decision. Sometimes it is this unsettlement in the pits of our stomach that we cannot quite put our finger on, but it is there tugging away at us. It is a sense of urgency and not hurry. For urgent matters are handled with an intentional strategy and a relentless posture to answer the immediate need at hand. What good is it to stand at an automatic door that opens in recognition of your presence if you will not walk in it? Your purpose is presenting you an open door of honoring God, doing Kingdom business, and blessing a multitude. Take heart that the present moment is all you have; it is the precious aspect of time. Now, greater than ever before, is your time to possess the land.

**Daily Declaration**
"Let me hear of Your unfailing love each morning, for I am trusting You. Show me where to walk, for I give myself to You."

**Prayer**
Son of the living God, you are my Lord and my Savior. Forgive me

Father for operating in a manner of delay and not one of "now". I asked that you show what it is that You desire for me to do now for the Kingdom. I relinquish this false sense of control and give you full reigns over every area of my life. I bend my ear and open my heart towards Your instructions. You are Jehovah Shammah; for You are there Lord to lead me in your ways. Guide my footsteps according to Your divine will for my life. I pray that for wise counsel and a posture to receive it even when it may be a harsh truth. I do not want to be wise in my own eyes and delay all that You have in store for me. I am a Kingdom kid on a Kingdom assignment; and for that I am honored to serve.

You and Your people. I desire to walk in Your love and truth; knowing that I have a fail proof life serving You. Thanks for keeping me for such a time as this to bring glory to Your Kingdom. I will seek to operate in the power of now. In Jesus' name. Amen.

Today's Song Selection
"I'll Just Say Yes" - Brian Courtney Wilson

**Moment of Reflection**
1. What am I grateful to God for today?
2. How did I "Live in It" for my purpose today?
3. What did today's chapter reveal to me?
4. Did I allow God to be in control or did I allow myself to be my own God today? How did I or how did I not surrender control?

Let me hear of Your unfailing ♡ love each morning, for I am trusting You. Show me where to walk, for I give myself to You.

PSALM 143:8 NLT

DAY 16

# From This to That

> "I pray that God, the source of hope, will fill you completely with joy and peace because you trust in him. Then you will overflow with confident hope through the power of the Holy Spirit."
>
> Romans 15:23

As you walk in your purpose you are in a process of transformation. This takes time and patience. Many believe that the process is about the manifestation of the destination, but quite frankly the beauty is in the transformation that takes place over time in the journey. Do not be so destiny-minded that you miss the significance of your submission to God's appointed timing for your purpose to be fulfilled. The gifts of peace, rest, and joy are wrapped up in submitting to God's timetable. Secondly, do not allow people's inability to see your vision discourage you from what God has purposed for you to do. The vision was given to you, not others. If I were to give you my eyeglasses with its specific prescriptive lenses for my eyesight, you would struggle to see what I can see when I wear them. Your vision is like a newborn baby; everyone knows that a newborn does not get passed from hand to hand because of the possibility of germ contamination from unclean hands. Just as with your vision, you cannot casually pass it around in discussion with others - especially with those with small thinking. People's shortsighted view will create the contamination of doubt and fear; leading you to question what you heard God said to you.

I am a proud member of Delta Sigma Theta Sorority, Inc.; a service organization of sisterhood and scholarship founded on Christian principles by twenty-two illustrious trailblazing collegiate African American women on the campus of Howard University in Washington. D.C. While going through the process, my line sister (also known as my pledge sister) preached a message for our pledge line and our big sisters. The title of her message was, "From This to That...". The sermon specifically outlined that every experience we encounter will take us from a preparation state to a manifestation posture. The process at times may seem bleak—as if God has forgotten about us. But it is those times you hold on even more as our God is good all of time. Knowing His magnitude of love for us will ease our troubled mind in the journey. You had to *grow* from this to *receive* that which God has purposed for you. From this to that is the surrendered trust walk we take with our Abba Father through every season of life.

As you move from "this to that" it will require a mindset change, divine partnerships, and an obedient attitude. What may look unconventional and/or unreasonable is the very thing God is using to elevate you in your purpose. Fear not, you are right where you need to be. The enemy will present fear as a distraction to take you off course. Think about the purpose of the scarecrow the farmer uses amongst his/her crops. The scarecrow is used to produce fear in the crows to deter them from eating the best crops. You protect what has value; your purpose has great value. Do not allow the devil's scarecrow to keep you in fear from going after God's best crops. A wise crow knows that the scary image being presented is a clear indication that something good is blocked by an obstacle of lies to discourage the crow from pursuing the *good thing*! You are building for a future that is nurtured by the faith walk you take today. What are you feeding your future? In the words of one of my favorite entertainers, Jasmine Guy, "Do the things you are afraid of..." The process of living in your purpose is not the absence of fear; it is acceptance of faith. You must run to the sound of the roar because the very thing you are afraid of reveals your greatest opportunity. It is being vulnerable to change so that God can help you to succeed in your purpose lacking nothing. It is that *now* thing to get you to your destined purpose.

"Living in it" is a lifestyle of serving God with your whole heart, holding His hand in the rough patches of life, and living a holy and peaceable life full of expectation of God's abundance. It is the essence of finally coming into agreement with God and believing He will do what He said He would do through you. Living in it will teach you that sometimes you just have to shut up. Constant rehearsals of describing a negative emotional state will keep your focus on impossibilities instead of God's great possibilities.

Feelings are temporal, but the words you speak can last a lifetime. Find pleasure in your "from this to that" process. Whatever He was, He is. Whatever He said, He will do. Whatever He declared; He will make it so. Know that you have true assurance in God!

Your provision always awaits your obedience. The act of obedience helps you to know the blessing of God as your anchor. Since God is the Master Orchestrator who cares about your success in living in your purpose, He will intentionally remove "idols" in your life. God is saying you will *not* have any false gods that were never created to support you to be your dependent source. He is *the source*—period! God will shut down the sky to give you Heaven. You cannot stay here you have to get "there"—there is the place of obedience (from this to that). Sometimes God will guide you with what He withholds from you to move you to the next level so that you don't have a dependency on a support system that does not have its source in Him. Stay where God plants you but be nimble enough to go from this to that when He is ready to elevate you in your purpose.

**Daily Declaration**
"Let me hear of Your unfailing love each morning, for I am trusting You. Show me where to walk, for I give myself to You."

**Prayer**
Gracious and merciful Messiah. You are the Light of the World. Yahweh, the I Am, You are my everything. I just want to say thank You. Thank You for allowing me to enter my awakening; awakening of my purpose that is far greater than me. You have kept me every

step of the way as You have allowed me to witness Your unchanging hand and steadfast love upon my life. Yes, you have taken me from this to that to be a vessel for Your kingdom. I humbly thank You. I say yes Lord to Your will and to Your way; letting go of fear that stifles my trust walk with You. Lord, Father, God You are my strength, my peace, and my Savior. Show me how to best honor You through this temple which You have set up within me. Guide me in my eating habits, in my entertainment choices and even in what I wear so that your house that I may glorify you in all that I do and not cause my brothers and sisters to stumble. I will live in my purpose from this day forward. In Jesus' name. Amen.

**Today's Song Selection**
"Spirit Break Out" - William McDowell ft. Trinity Anderson

**Moment of Reflection**
1. What am I grateful to God for today?
2. How did I "Live in It" for my purpose today?
3. What did today's chapter reveal to me?
4. Did I allow God to be in control or did I allow myself to be my own God today? How did I or how did I not surrender control?

DAY 17

# The Benediction: Keys to Evolving in Your Purpose

*"Give your complete attention to these matters. Throw yourself into your tasks so that everyone will see your progress. Keep a close watch on how you live and on your teaching. Stay true to what is right for the sake of your own salvation and the salvation of those who hear you."*
*1 Timothy 4:15-16*

In life you will experience ups and downs. You will meet new people, as well as, let go of a few people. But just know that every moment you have spent on Earth has been a gift. What I want you to do with this gift is to share it with someone else—whether it be giving someone a smile, lending a servant hand, or sharing a word of encouragement. Use your gift to be a blessing. The world is your playground; either you take a seat on the swing-set of life or you sit on the bench and watch life pass you by. Do not be afraid of taking risks. Risks are blessed opportunities wrapped in the unknown. You will never experience increase or optimal fulfillment if you are controlled by your fears.

Each day will be a building block added to your purpose. There is no cookie-cutter answer or process that guarantees your success; only your obedience to the Word of God and your commitment to stay the course with a faithful attitude will ensure God's perfect will to be manifested in your life. Ultimate success is being in the sweet spot of God's will. I will be the first to say being in God's perfect will for your life will not always feel like it. There will be times you will question whether you heard from God; and if what you heard was true. Seek out wise counsel by praying to God and asking Him to lead you to the right people to speak into your life. The reason for this is because doing life alone can leave you depleted and discouraged. Not only should you seek out wise counsel, but literally step out on faith on what you felt in your heart to do. At times, our desire to get it right leaves us immobilized from doing anything at all. I honestly believe whether it is the right move, God is with us and is very capable of redeeming misstep for His glory. God sees your heart of faith and will not penalize your faith-in-training maneuvers. Try to have a receptive heart and mind to receive God's instructions even when the commands may not make sense or feel good.

The beautiful thing about your purpose at it evolves is that it draws you closer to your Creator, aligning you to His will, love, and peace. As your purpose develops over time, take into consideration the following keys to keep you in alignment:

- Know your purpose Jeremiah 29:11 - recognizing why God has called you to this path
- Find Your Soil to Plant in Ps. 92:12-15 - knowing whom and where you will serve

- Trust the Process Gen 8:22 - keeping God at the helm of your journey to remain steadfast in all seasons of life.

As you matriculate in your purpose, it is imperative to remain humble and attentive to God's promptings. Do not yearn for the mantle to be raved by other people and lose your foundational focus on God's leading. If you lose sight of this, then pride and haughtiness can set in which can lead to the demise of your calling. As a result, you will define your identity by the applause of others, rather than the applause of God. Be open to the move of God's hands. There is a special feeling of comfort when you remain flexible and maintain a peaceful disposition as you progress in your purpose. This is done by having faith in the Father and not circumstances; the kind of faith that only comes from spending intimate time with Him daily. You must be in a posture to "faith your fears"; acknowledging that fear is present within you but using it as fuel to propel you. Faith gives us the right perspective when you make it your mental resolute.

As you pursue your purpose, allow this to be your motivation: God gave it to you, and it is yours to go get it! God has not changed His mind towards you. Speak boldly. Expect abundantly. Know that at the very core your purpose is ultimately to do God's will for your life.

It is easy to feel dismayed when you feel engulfed with stressful situations, casting a fog over your purpose. As you commit to an intentional time of devotion with God your faith will be strengthened, and your vision restored through His written word. He has given you grace for your purpose and provision to live in it. I want to leave you with this thought: Jesus Christ died for you, so

I want to leave you with this thought: Jesus Christ died for you, so why not live for Him?

**Daily Declaration**

"Let me hear of Your unfailing love each morning, for I am trusting You. Show me where to walk, for I give myself to You."

**Prayer**

Heavenly Father. Lord God holy is Your name. You are Jehovah Ori; the Lord my light illuminating my pathway. God you are bigger than any trial, disappointment, or mistake that I may face. As I relinquish control to gain control of my life through You Lord, I pray for the gift of faith to be encouraged through the journey. Remind me of Your unfailing love that has never failed me yet. Every time I look around I see how much you have favored me. God, I want to thank You for keeping me. Touch me oh Abba Father so that I can be more like You. Change me in order to be used by You. Change the motivations of my heart to be aligned to Your heart, God. I surrender to the process of transformation. Father, I pray for a fresh outpour of anointing to run this race. Strengthen my sails that I may have the spirit of Elijah to not only live in my purpose, but to do it with excellence. Be glorified Jesus. You are worthy of all my praise. In Jesus' name I do pray. Amen

**Today's song selection:**
"Big" – Pastor Mike, Jr.

**Moment of Reflection**
1. What am I grateful to God for today?
2. How did I "Live in It" for my purpose today?
3. What did today's chapter reveal to me?
4. Did I allow God to be in control or did I allow myself to be my own God today? How did I or how did I not surrender control?

# CREDITS

Brittany Craveiro
*Illustrator*

www.ingramcontent.com/pod-product-compliance
Lightning Source LLC
Chambersburg PA
CBHW070936160426
**43193CB00011B/1699**